Telling Our Faith Story

Janice Price

Illustrations by Taffy Davis

Board of Mission Occasional Paper No. 8

CHURCH HOUSE
PUBLISHING

Church House Publishing
Church House
Great Smith Street
London
SW1P 3NZ

ISBN 0 7151 5543 1

Published 1999 for the Board of Mission of the Church of England
by Church House Publishing

This report has only the authority of the working group which produced it.

Acknowledgement

Chapter 2, 'Telling Our Faith Story' is based (with adaptations)
on *God's Story, Our Story: How We Share Faith as Women* (pp. 53–69),
copyright © The Mothers' Union 1998 and reproduced by permis-
sion.

Cover design by Image-On Artworks
Printed in England by Halstan & Co. Ltd

Contents

Foreword

Evangelism now has a growing place on the agenda of the Christian Church. Research continues to indicate that most people come to faith in Christ through meeting and relating to other Christians. But many church members still find it difficult to talk about their faith.

The purpose of this booklet is to give help and guidance in overcoming barriers which can inhibit the telling of faith stories. Telling our story must always begin with our own personal experience of God; but conveying it requires the building up of relationship and trust with others. Only then does it become appropriate to share with them the difference which Christ's love has made in our lives. Such faith is always more than merely personal and individual. Our stories belong to the life and witness of the whole Church.

I welcome *Telling Our Faith Story* and commend it to churches, organizations and groups who want to be better equipped to speak about the love of God in Christ.

✠ Nigel McCulloch
Bishop of Wakefield

Introduction

Welcome to *Telling Our Faith Story*. When we talk about communicating the Christian faith there are two stories to tell. There is the story of our personal faith journey when we talk about the stages we have passed through and the events and experiences that have happened to us. Then, if we call ourselves Christians, there is also the wider story of the Christian faith seen in what God has done through Jesus Christ. These two stories interweave and interlock and are inextricably linked. This booklet is about telling these two stories with the purpose of encouraging others to follow Jesus.

In my experience many Christians would like to be able to talk about their faith in a relaxed and open way. Yet, few find this easy. *Telling Our Faith Story* is a process designed to help and encourage Christians to speak about their experiences of faith. In other words, to get the story of Jesus on to the lips of his followers.

The activities suggested in this booklet provide a starting point for fuller learning in the Christian faith. It is not an end in itself. It is hoped that these exercises will whet the appetite for more. After these activities it is likely that Christians may want to do a further course and discover more about their faith and continue to grow in confidence in telling their story and reasoning their faith with those who are not Christians. The Resources section at the back of this booklet gives further information.

Telling Our Faith Story has been tried and tested in many different contexts – urban, rural and suburban churches and groups. It has been found to be a useful tool in getting the gospel on to the lips of Christians. There are many ways to tell our faith story and this is only one method. It is important that as this process is used it is adapted to suit different contexts.

1

Stories

Many people meet the Christian faith through stories. They may first hear the Christian story through the school nativity play or through watching television. Also, many people hear the story of Jesus through somebody who calls themself a Christian. To encounter the Christian faith is to encounter the story of what God has done through Jesus Christ.

Stories surround us at every point of life. They are a universal phenomenon. Whether they are the fairy stories we meet in childhood or television soap operas, or the stories we hear on the news every day, we cannot escape them.

But, what do we mean when we describe something as a story? There are many different types of stories but broadly they fall into two categories – factual and imagined. In other words, stories are based on real or imaginary events. The stories we hear every day on the news, or the stories we hear from the past, are based on events that actually happened – they are history. They are records of events and happenings. The story of Jesus Christ falls into this category. The Christian faith, which is the story of Jesus, is a record of a man who lived in first-century Roman-occupied Palestine, who died a tragic death and then, miraculously, rose from the dead and, Christians believe, lives today. This is what is meant by Christianity being an historical religion.

Imaginary stories are those stories which are not based on historical fact but have their origins in the mind of the writer or in other sources. They can be powerful, entertaining and fascinating with wide appeal. These types of stories also hold and convey truths about human life. Into this category come stories such as children's fairy stories, novels, soap operas, films and so on. Some seem closer to real life than others but they have a great power to grasp our imagination.

Whether stories are real or imagined they help us to make sense of the lives we live. That's why we find them so fascinating. Stories provide a safe place, outside of ourselves, through which we try to work out our hopes and dreams, conflicts and dilemmas, whether or not we realize we are doing it. They express, at a deep level, some of the questions we have about life and the way we live it. They can also give us hope to believe that there is a better world.

Stories are an essential part of who we are – our identity. Shared stories help us to create what we are. A shared story of grief, threat, oppression or joy can bring people together and acknowledge what they hold in common. This has tremendous creative force. Today, we are beginning to hear many of the stories of oppressed peoples. For them, an important part of discovering their cultural identity is about rediscovering the stories that were lost by being under the control of an oppressor. Examples of this are stories from the native Americans of the USA and Canada or the peoples of South America or, closer to home, the Celtic stories.

So far, we have looked at stories on a large scale, at those stories which we hold in common. But stories work at a smaller or more personal level too. Each of us has our own story of life. It is an on-going story. It is a journey, a pilgrimage. Our story is based on our own life-choices and decisions, the things that happen to us, and what we do to others, as well as the people who influence us. For Christians the key part of the story is our relationship with God in Jesus Christ and with other Christians. It is this story that we are focusing on here.

The writers of the books of the Bible used many different types and styles of story. The early books of the Old Testament contain the history of the people of Israel. These books tell the story of the people of Israel and their relationship with God. The use of the word 'history' here reflects the style of the story and is not nec-essarily a judgement on whether or not the stories are literally true. The Old Testament is also full of prophecy and poetry, often used together, to tell the story of Israel and the love that God has for them and of his desire that they follow his laws. These stories are rich in images and convey God's love for his people.

In the New Testament we have the story (or stories) about Jesus found in the Gospels. Each Gospel tells the story of Jesus with a different focus. St Matthew's Gospel, for example, focuses on telling the story for a Jewish audience. Luke, in contrast, is seen as the writer who wants to tell the story of Jesus for Gentiles and marginalized peoples. This differing focus is shown through the choice of events recalled and stories told. The Gospels are a good example of the basic rule of communication – think of your audience first and foremost. That is why we need not worry when we choose different parts of our story to tell to others. What we tell has to be relevant to our hearers.

The Epistles tell the story of certain churches who have particular concerns and problems and who need the help of the leaders of the early Church. We read their story through letters that were sent to them.

Jesus, too, used stories to communicate the message of the kingdom of God. He often used parables to express a certain aspect of the kingdom. He told many different parables because there are many aspects of the kingdom. Jesus regularly illustrated his teachings through the use of stories. For example, the Good Samaritan is a story illustrating Jesus' teaching on loving your neighbour. Also, the story or parable of the lost sheep shows Jesus answering a question from the Pharisees about why he was associating with sinners. There are many other examples. What is important to note here is that the telling of stories is an important way of conveying the truth about the Christian gospel. But the story is not an end in itself. It points towards who God is and how we relate to God. That was true in the stories Jesus told and is also the key feature of why we tell our story today.

Telling Our Faith Story is about telling the story of Jesus through our own story and that of the Church. People find each other's stories and experiences fascinating. To tell our faith story means expressing how faith in God works for us today. People need to know that the Christian faith is real, living and relevant. People often need to see that faith works before they show any interest in it as a way to live. This does not mean that once we have a relationship with God all will be happy ever after. Not at all. What is important for many people today is that faith is seen to be relevant in the dark and painful times of life as well as the good times.

Every Christian has a story to tell. The problem is that so often we don't realize it, or think that our story and our experience cannot possibly be interesting or relevant to someone who is not a Christian. In fact, the reverse is true. In many people's experience it is hearing about someone's journey of faith that prompts the question 'what about me?' There is also great value in telling our faith story within the church community. Other people's stories of faith are a source of great encouragement, comfort and strength as we see how God is at work in the lives of other Christians. Telling these stories also helps to build up the Christian community. Such shared witness is the evidence of God's grace and power living within his people. The exercises in the next chapter will help you to find and express your story of faith in different ways.

Why learn to tell our story? The purpose of telling our faith story is to point others towards faith in God through Jesus Christ and what he has done for us. It is not to make us seem clever or especially religious. It is about being realistic about the ups and downs, the joys and sorrows of life and how God in Jesus travels this way with us. It is also to make us think and pray about where we go next. How can we grow in our relationship with God in the future?

If we call ourselves Christians our story does not stand on its own but is part of the bigger story of what God has done through Jesus Christ. It is as if we are telling two stories that are inextricably linked – our story and the story of Jesus. Here we are using our story to open the story of God to others.

The Church is entrusted with the task of telling the story of Jesus to a world that God loves and wants to save. The Church tells God's story in many ways – through worship and the liturgy which contains both the Word of God and the sacrament. The story is told through the meeting of Word and symbol, primarily and supremely through the Eucharist. It is here that Word and symbol work together to tell the story of Jesus. As we hear the story of Jesus from Scripture so it is enacted through the symbols of bread and wine in the Eucharist. It's rather like the road to Emmaus where those travelling with Jesus realized who he was when he broke bread. It was as though all he had been saying on the journey fitted into place at that moment.

The story is also told through the life of the people of God – the Church – as it lives the life of God the Holy Trinity through worship and living as Christians in the world. It tells the story through the lives of its members as they witness to the love of God in Jesus Christ in what they say and what they do.

We are all called to tell the story. Let's now look at how we can be more effective in doing just that.

2
Telling Our Faith Story

'It had never occurred to me that I had a faith story to tell. But when I started to think about it I had quite a lot to say.'

'I was really nervous about talking about my life and faith. It has always been a very private part of me but after the exercise I felt really good, particularly when others told me that what I had said meant something to them too.'

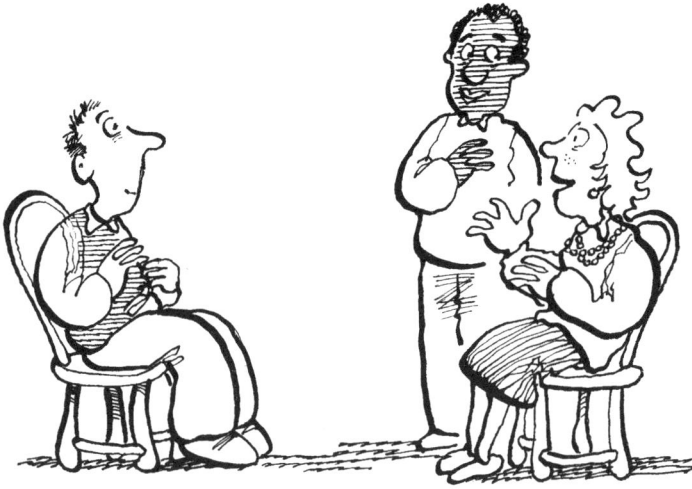

These are the reactions of two people who have taken part in a *Telling Our Faith Story* exercise. Despite feeling some anxiety about talking about their faith, having completed the exercise they felt positive about the value of their story. Others have said that they felt affirmed and confident after the exercise and encouraged to use their story to tell others about their experiences of God.

Telling Our Faith Story can be a liberating experience even though it may seem daunting at first. After all, it may be the first time that anything like this has been attempted. Such an exercise may raise all sorts of uncertainties and questions and painful times that are difficult to deal with. Talking about our faith means we open ourselves to others and become vulnerable. But working through this exercise can raise our confidence about telling others about the Christian faith and what it means to us. This exercise has been designed carefully to provide a safe place for the first attempts to tell our story. It has been tried and tested and, if possible, should be worked through as a whole. Each part of the exercise has a purpose which is explained in the instructions. However, the leader may find other ways of doing the exercise that they feel is more appropriate to their context. If so, adapt as is necessary. With careful and sensitive leading people can find confidence and affirmation to tell their story. Here goes!

What is required?

The basic requirements are:

- a group of people who are wanting to develop their confidence in faith-sharing;
- someone to lead the exercise;
- a room or rooms big enough for people to break into groups of three with enough space so that group discussions cannot be overheard.

It is a good rule to have no fewer than three groups working in any one room. If there are only two groups it is very easy to overhear and be distracted. Equally with more than three groups similar problems can be encountered through too much background noise.

This is an exercise that can be used with people who have been Christians for a short time or a longer period. It can be used with young and older people, clergy and lay people, women and men. It has been found to be a good exercise to use with mixed groups of, for example, younger and older people. It has been found to be a good way to share experiences and to learn to respect each other. Telling our faith stories actually helps to build community. We see each other as real people and not just in our Sunday church mode. We may have some surprises! It has been used in rural, urban and suburban groups and churches of all denominations.

The role of the leader is crucial to the effectiveness of the group. It is the job of the leader to encourage people to take part in the exercise and to attempt to allay any anxieties. It is good, but not essential, if the leader has already done the exercise. The leader needs to allow plenty of time for people to express their questions and anxieties as well as their hopes during the course of the exercise. Those taking part should not feel steam-rollered into something they don't want to do. Like any group exercise, the full benefit of the process will not be obtained if participants are wondering whether or not they actually want to take part. The leader needs to create a warm, supportive and affirming atmosphere. If the leader has done the exercise, then it may be a good idea to tell the group briefly how they felt, both at the beginning and when they had completed it. The leader does not need to be an expert but a facilitator – helping others to get the most out of the exercise.

Here is the suggested programme for a *Telling Our Faith Story* exercise and a commentary on the various parts of the exercise. This provides group leaders especially with a guide to the process of *Telling Our Faith Story*. If possible, let each member of the group have a copy of this commentary so that they can refer to it in the course of the exercise.

Timing

It is important not to rush those taking part. Allow sufficient time for participants to grasp the information they need, ask any questions and do the exercises. Here are some suggested timings.

Welcome – leader (5 minutes)

Introduction to exercise – leader (20 minutes)

What interests me? – activity (10 minutes)

Preparatory work – personal work (20–30 minutes)

Sharing our stories – group exercise (30 minutes)

Feedback and reflection (10 minutes)

Growing our stories (15 minutes)

Welcome

A good welcome is one of the most important parts of any event or exercise. At the moment the participant walks through the door they will begin to pick up the atmosphere of the place and occasion. Make sure there is someone to welcome people and to give out any relevant information. The leaders and organizers need to be relaxed. If people see the organizers rushing around this will give the impression of bad organization and of an event where people are far from confident and relaxed. The leader should be in place early enough to welcome others. If a large group is meeting, get others to help with the welcoming. A good welcome is the art of helping people to feel accepted and affirmed but not swamping them with good-will.

Introductory session

The purpose of this session is to introduce participants to the whole exercise. First, participants should be made aware of the purpose of the exercise – to build their confidence in telling their faith story. Secondly, participants should be introduced briefly to the programme and the various elements and timings. It is not necessary here to introduce each part in detail – that can wait until you are about to do each part. This is a good point to pray, asking for God's blessing on the exercise.

It is also necessary at this point for the leader to introduce participants to the importance of stories. The points made in Chapter 1 will help leaders to convey this. Try to ensure that you begin on a positive note. One way of doing this is to ask people what their favourite stories are and why. Also, ask the group which soap operas they watch or listen to. Get a few people to share briefly their responses. Go on to explain the Christian story and how our personal stories link in with the bigger picture of the story of God – Father, Son and Holy Spirit. In other words, explain how we have our personal stories and experiences but how we also inhabit the bigger story of God in creation which is told and re-told by the

Church in the power of the Holy Spirit. This introduction needs to be concluded with an explanation of the next part of the exercise – What interests me?

What interests me?

The purpose of this exercise is to encourage people to talk about themselves through their interests. This will help them to begin on a positive theme which will raise their confidence before embarking on the more difficult task of talking about their experiences of faith. There is no limit to the range of subject matter. Gardening, motorbikes, bees, cricket and 'EastEnders' have all been covered in this part of the exercise – and many others! There is no need to take feedback from this exercise. This activity is a useful way to begin the speaking and listening process that the *Telling Our Faith Story* exercise needs in order to be successful.

Get those participating into groups of three. Each member of the group can talk for up to three minutes on any subject that interests them. It is important to appoint a time-keeper who will keep each speaker to time. If the speaker uses less than three minutes, then others in the group can ask questions.

Preparing to share our story

It is suggested that this part of the exercise is done by individuals on their own and in silence. The time should be used to reflect on their

own story and how they are going to present it. To begin with, however, the group leader has the vital task of introducing the main part of the whole exercise – sharing our stories in small groups. This is what participants are preparing for. At this point the group leader needs to do two important things – first, to set the ground rules or guidelines for the exercise and secondly, to introduce participants to the different ways they can think about and then tell their story to others. The order in which the various parts of the exercise are undertaken can be varied. A leader may feel it is better to begin the exercise with the section on 'God's story' and approach 'My story' at a later time.

Setting the ground rules

The leader should make these points to the whole group.

- The object of the exercise is to build the confidence of Christians to share their faith story with others.

- In sharing our faith story there are no rights or wrongs. All experience is valid and to be respected. It may be that this is the first time a person has articulated their faith story and negative or critical comments can destroy confidence. This is not a test in doctrine or theology. It is sharing what God has done in our lives.

- Each person who is sharing their faith story is in control of what they say. They choose what they are going to share and how. They are under no obligation to share what does not feel appropriate for them.

- While a person is sharing their story there should be no interruptions or questions unless these are invited by the person who is talking. They also have the option not to answer questions if they feel they are inappropriate.

- It is possible that doing this exercise may raise painful and difficult memories, in particular of loss and grief. After all, it is often in the difficult and painful times that we grow most in our faith. It is important for the group to hear the pain of those sharing and to pray for them, if that is what they would like.

● Confidentiality is a general rule for this exercise and should be respected.

● This exercise is as much about how we listen as how we tell our faith story. Listening is about being open to what the other person has to say. It is about hearing without judging and about valuing what is said. In this exercise we are both telling and listening.

After the group leader has shared these with the wider group, the leader should ask for general agreement from the group to these ground rules and ask if there are any further things that should be added. Remember to give adequate time for questions from the group. Participants will be asked to get into groups of three. Each person in the group will have up to ten minutes to share their faith story.

Part one – my story

Now explain to the group that before they tell their story in groups they are to have a time of silent personal preparation. This should take about twenty minutes – or longer if it is possible. Participants have a lot of work to do in this time.

The leader should then outline to the participants the various ways in which they can prepare to tell their story. There are many ways this can be done and participants should be encouraged to use the method which appeals to them most. Participants can use one of the following three methods.

1. QUESTIONS

Participants can use some or all of the following questions to reflect on their faith journey. They can then use their answers to the questions to share with others in their group of three.

- Which people or experiences have most influenced my own faith journey?
- What are the milestones in my faith journey?
- When did I first become aware of God in my life?
- How has this awareness developed?
- What are the things about Jesus that make him special to me?
- How have I experienced the Holy Spirit in my life and what difference has this made?
- What difference has my faith made in my life recently?
- What place does the Church play in my faith journey?
- Have there been times when God has seemed absent?
- How did I learn from these times?
- What doubts and questions remain with me, and what certainties support me in my journey of faith?

2. IMAGES

Participants can use a time-line or grid to plot their story of faith. Take a piece of paper and draw the following:

[_____]

Taking the left-hand bracket as the beginning point and the right-hand bracket as the point reached now, plot the course of the faith journey. Different colours can be used to indicate the character or mood of the time. For example, red for the high spots and blue for the difficult and painful times. Use the small group time to explain the various points and phases of the journey.

Participants may feel that their journey is more appropriately expressed as a series of interlocking circles. Draw circles to describe the various points of the faith journey and use words and/or colours to explain what they represent. Try to explain, too, what was happening when the circles interlock.

Also, it would be possible simply to draw the images that the various points on your faith journey bring to mind. Again, use colours to indicate the feelings and moods of the various phases of the journey.

3. FINISH THE SENTENCE

Finish the sentence 'My faith journey has been like . . .'

The completed sentence then describes what the journey has been like. It is most likely that everyone can think of a number of different ways to finish the sentence. If so, all of them can be written down and shared in the small group time.

If you are doing Parts one and two on separate occasions, get participants into groups of three now. Go to page 19 for instructions for group work.

When participants have completed this part of the exercise get everyone together into the large group. This is an important time for getting people's reaction to what they have done and answering any questions. Here are some suggestions about handling feedback. Take reactions and write them on a flip chart if this is appropriate.

●   Ask for immediate reactions to the exercise. How did they feel before and now that they have completed the exercise?

- Give participants a few minutes of silence to write down their thoughts and feelings. Then ask for volunteers to share what they have written.

- Ask participants to share with their neighbour their reactions to the exercise. Then share their thoughts with the wider group if they want to.

The following questions may help with feedback.

- How do you think and feel now you have completed the exercise?

- Have you done anything like this before today?

- What was positive about the exercise?

- What would you have done differently?

You can now move on to the next part of the exercise. It is possible to do Parts one and two together. However, if time is limited it may be better to do Part one and Part two on separate occasions.

Part two – my story and God's story

It is important to recognize the different ways in which our story links in with God's bigger story. The exercise above helps us to realize the path our own journey of faith has taken. However, the Christian journey is not an isolated journey but one that we take with others. We journey with the Christian community through belonging to the Church. That brings us into contact with the bigger story of God – Father, Son and Holy Spirit. To be a Christian it is necessary to see our faith story as part of the story of God. The key questions are, 'how do I link in with the wider story of God?' or, 'how do I see my story as part of God's story?' Use some of the

preparation time to consider these questions. The following exercises may help participants to think about this. It would be a good idea for participants to have these pages with them as they prepare.

PEOPLE

With which character or characters in the Bible or in history do you identify? Write down or draw the reason why these people are so important and explain where your stories are similar and where they are different. How do the lives of Christians in the past challenge the way we live the Christian faith today?

PASSAGES

Think of any passage or passages in the Bible that have been important to you at a time or times in your journey. In the small group be prepared to say something about why they are important and have challenged or helped you at a particular stage. What do they tell you about Jesus and what following him means?

PSALMS

Look at Psalm 23. It is a remarkable Psalm because it describes many of the things we experience along our journey. It talks of the times when we have plenty and the dark times when despair is near. Using the Psalm, describe the times when these different things have happened to you. Above all, what have you learnt about God in these times? How has being part of the Church, the people of God, helped or hindered in these different phases of the journey?

PLACES

Is there a place where you know the presence of God in a special way? How does this place or places help you to see your story as part of God's story? What have these places taught you about the Christian faith? For example, many people remember pilgrimages to places like Walsingham as important times in their journey. Or a visit to a conference like Spring Harvest may have been a significant milestone. For some people the special place where they know the presence of God is in a place of natural beauty or even where the dog is walked.

SYMBOLS AND SEASONS

The Christian faith is full of symbols. These symbols point to the love of God in Christ. They are not ends in themselves but point to the greater truth about what God has done for us in Christ. Celebrating the various seasons in the Christian year helps us to see the story of God – Father, Son and Holy Spirit as a whole. After all, you can't have the resurrection without the cross. What symbols or seasons in the Christian Church help you to see your story as part of the whole story of Jesus? Have different symbols or seasons become important to you at different times in your journey? Reflect on how these times have enabled your faith to grow and develop.

MUSIC, IMAGES AND OBJECTS

The Christian faith has provided the inspiration for countless outstanding works of art whether in images or sound. Often these can become important markers for us in our understanding of our life and faith. Think of the pieces of music, hymns or songs that are important for you. Ask yourself why these have been important at a particular time. Think in the same way of pictures or any objects that are significant for you. How has what they represent helped you to grow in the Christian faith?

Group work – telling our faith story

Get participants into groups of three. When in groups ask each group to appoint a time-keeper. Each member of the group has a maximum of ten minutes in which to tell their faith story using the material they prepared in the preparation period. The job of the time-keeper is to ensure that everyone gets their time to tell their story. It is designed both to give space and time to those who need it and to control those who would speak for too long! It is possible that some participants do not find enough to say for the whole ten minutes. If that is the case they may welcome questions. If not, move on to the next person. If all members of the group have told their story then discuss the similarities and differences in the stories. Tell each other what has been encouraging and surprising about their story of faith.

When all the groups have completed the three contributions the group leader should ask everyone to come together as a whole group for feedback and reflection on the exercise.

Feedback and reflection

Feedback from the exercise can be taken in a variety of ways. Here are some suggestions.

- Ask for participants' immediate reactions to the exercise. How did they feel before and how do they feel now they have completed the exercise? Take reactions from the group and write them up on a flip chart.

- Give participants a few minutes of silence to write down their thoughts and feelings about the exercise. Then ask for volunteers to share what they have written.

- Ask participants to share with their neighbour their reactions to the exercise. Then share their thoughts with the wider group.

The following questions may help with feedback.

- How do you think and feel now you have completed this exercise?

- Have you done anything like this before today?

- What was positive about the exercise?

- What would you have done differently?

Growing our stories

The final part of the exercise is about how we grow in our faith as Christians. The key points to be made in this part of the process are:

- As Christians we should *never think 'I've arrived.'* There is always more to know about God and our journey or pilgrimage. Just as we tend a plant, so our relationship with God in Christ needs to be cared for and tended. The way we do this is primarily through worship. By this we mean worship in the whole of life, on Monday as well as Sunday. Worship means directing the whole of our lives towards God, as a plant grows towards the light.

- We should *use our stories.* If faith in God gives meaning to our lives then be prepared to tell others that this is so. There is no set script. As we grow as people in faith so we have more to tell. Change is part of life and our stories will take sometimes surprising twists and turns. In the end, we need to be able to give an answer to the question, 'what difference does your faith make to your life?' And, we are not on our own. The Holy Spirit will give us the words to say.

● It is important to *watch our language*. It's easy to talk to other Christians in the language of our Christian faith. However, this means nothing to those who are not Christians. In other words, don't use jargon. Imagine what a person who is not a Christian makes of phrases like 'washed in the blood of the lamb' or 'catechesis'? Remember, the first rule of communication is 'know your audience'. Share what is relevant to the people we want to communicate with.

Prayer and worship

At the conclusion of the exercise, it is important to pray and worship God. Give some time for silent prayer and worship as well as praying as a group. Some Bible readings that could be used at this point include:

> John 1.35-42 (Jesus calls his first disciples)
>
> Luke 24.13-34 (the road to Emmaus)

Use the following prayer, if appropriate.

> Father, Son and Holy Spirit,
> Thank you for being with me,
> For the times that have been good
> And the times that have been difficult.
> Help me to grow in my knowledge of you
> And to tell others about your love. Amen.

3
What Next?

Being human is all about change, development and becoming more of what God has made us to be. In other words, there are always new things to tell, new experiences to recount, new things to know. Being a Christian is about growing in our love of God and for the world he has made. It is about seeing ourselves as part of God's mission to the world. Having taken the step of telling our story in this exercise, here are some ways we can develop our Christian understanding.

Continue telling our story

There are always new experiences to weave into our story as we journey through our lives. There is a constant need for us to reflect on our life experiences in the light of our faith. This is called integrating life and faith. As new things happen so we have new ways in which to talk about God's love for us. In church life it is important to make opportunities for people to tell their stories either in a formal group set up for this purpose or informally. Then, when the opportunity arises it is possible to tell these growing stories to those who are interested in the Christian faith.

Courses – retreats – conferences – pilgrimage

If these sound frightening, they aren't. There are many courses available, designed for all abilities, contexts and interests. Emmaus, Alpha, the Catechumenate are just three of differing styles and content. Or there are the famous Cursillo weekends which seek to deepen faith and witness. Many Church of England dioceses and other denominations organize their own courses for those who want to know more about the Christian faith.

Many people, not just Christians, find going on a retreat a way to recharge their batteries and deepen their faith. Retreats can be taken either as part of a group or alone, and led by a spiritual director or self-directed. The National Retreat Movement is an excellent resource. Look in the Resources section at the end of this booklet for their address. There are also many Christian holidays or conferences designed to help people develop in their faith. A popular way to develop our faith is to go on pilgrimage. Travelling alone or with a group to a holy place or site gives an opportunity to pray, reflect on our lives and allow God to speak to us.

Prayer – Bible reading – worship

As we are all aware, there is no substitute for regular prayer and Bible reading. There are many resources available to help with these vital aspects of growing as a Christian. Take a look in any Christian bookshop.

Last word

Whatever method of journeying we prefer, the purpose of our journey is the same as that expressed in the Letter to the Philippians:

> I keep working toward that day when I will finally be all that Christ Jesus saved me for and wants me to be.

> (Philippians 3.12, *New Living Translation*)

Resources

Contacts and addresses

Here are a few of the contacts and addresses that can help in taking some of these ideas further.

Alpha

Holy Trinity Brompton, Brompton Road, London SW7

Arthur Rank Centre

National Agricultural Centre, Stoneleigh Park, Warwickshire CV8 2LZ

Bible Society

Stonehill Green, Westlea, Swindon SN5 7DG

Board of Mission

Church House, Great Smith Street, London SW1P 3NZ

Catechumenate Network

Canon Peter Ball, Whittonedge, Whittonditch Road, Ramsbury, Wiltshire SN8 2PX

Christian Enquiry Agency

Inter-Church House, 35–41 Lower Marsh, London SE1 7RL

Church Pastoral Aid Society

Athena Drive, Tachbrook Park, Warwick CV34 6NG

Mothers' Union

Mary Sumner House, 24 Tufton Street, London SW1P 3RB

National Retreat Association

The Central Hall, 256 Bermondsey Street, London SE1 3UJ

Springboard

4 Old Station Yard, Abingdon, Oxon OX14 3LD

Courses

The Alpha Course

Pioneered by Holy Trinity Brompton, a thirteen-week course exploring some of the basics of the Christian faith.

Credo

Written and presented by Bishop Lindsay Urwin, *Credo* provides an introduction to the Christian faith from an Anglo-Catholic perspective. *Credo* is published by the Church Union, Faith House, 7 Tufton Street, London SW1P 3QN.

Emmaus – The Way of Faith

A set of six resource books covering all aspects of the evangelistic process from initial contact through to growth as a Christian. Published by the National Society/Church House Publishing and available from Church House Bookshop (Tel: 0171-898 1301/1302; Fax: 0171-898 1305/1449; on-line catalogue: http://www.chpublishing.co.uk) and other Christian bookshops.

God's Story, Our Story

A Mothers' Union publication focusing on doing evangelism among women. Also published by the Mothers' Union are *To Live and Work* and *I Believe and Trust*. These are two courses designed to help Christians develop their understanding of their faith and role as witnesses to Jesus Christ.

Hidden Treasure and Discovering Hidden Treasure

Two videos, produced by the Arthur Rank Centre, which use the approach used in this booklet to encourage evangelism in rural areas. These videos have also been used in urban areas. Available from the Arthur Rank Centre.

How to Make Sense of God

Follows the journey of two young people as they seek God. Five videos with accompanying study material. Available from Poor Clare Community, Upper Aston Hall Lane, Hawarden, Clwyd CH5 3EN.

Lost for Words

A six-week course developed by the Church Pastoral Aid Society seeking to equip Christians to speak about their faith, covering many different aspects and issues in evangelism.